CW01594594

Hannah Jacobs

*with photographs by Chris Fairclough*

# BUILDING A MOTORWAY

Hamish Hamilton · London

The author and publishers would like to thank Fairclough Civil Engineering Ltd for all their help during the production of this book. Special thanks go to M. K. Eckersall, BSc, CEng, MICE, FIHT, Managing Director; A. J. Ellis, BSc, Deputy Project Manager; and K. Hick, FISTC, MSAI, AMIRT, Marketing Services Manager.

Fairclough Civil Engineering Ltd have kindly given permission to reproduce those photographs appearing on pages 10, 11, 13, 17.

Illustration by Gillian Hurry/Linda Rogers Associates

Design by Andrew Shoolbred

First published in Great Britain 1987 by
Hamish Hamilton Children's Books
27 Wrights Lane, London W8 5TZ
Copyright © 1987 by Hannah Jacobs (text)
Copyright © 1987 by Chris Fairclough (photographs)

Jacobs, Hannah
Building a motorway.
1. Express highways—Design and construction—Juvenile literature
I. Title
625.7 TE149

ISBN 0–241–11881–6

# Contents

# Introduction

The first section of motorway to be built in Britain was completed just under thirty years ago, near Preston in Lancashire. It was approximately 13 kilometres long, and in time became part of the M6 motorway linking Rugby and Carlisle. A year later, the first stretch of the M1 was built. This motorway was to become Britain's busiest, travelling due north from London to Leeds.

Today, motorways link most of Britain's major towns and cities, and form an essential part of its road system. They not only allow people and goods to travel quickly from one place to another; they also divert long-distance drivers from smaller roads and city centres, and so help local traffic to flow more smoothly.

The most recent motorway to be completed in Britain is the M25. You can see a plan of it on the opposite page. This motorway, 195 kilometres long, runs in a large ring around London. It was built in forty-one sections over a period of ten years, although the project was officially launched ten years before that. Fifteen of the country's top civil engineering contractors helped to build it. (A contractor makes an agreement with a client to do a particular job for an agreed price, within a fixed period of time.) One of the contractors was Fairclough Civil Engineering Ltd, who won the contract for the section between Leatherhead and Wisley in Surrey.

N
Wisley
Leatherhead

# The building contract

All public roads in Britain are built and maintained by the Government, and in particular by the Department of Transport (DTp for short). When a major new road is planned, the DTp can spend several years choosing a 'preferred route' and deciding how the road should be constructed. Once the plans have been published, many more months may go by while objections to the road are heard at a public enquiry. An independent inspector listens to the arguments on both sides and judges whether or not the road should be built.

If the DTp is given the go-ahead, a number of contractors are invited to put in their bids (known as tenders) for various sections of road. No one contractor is big enough to undertake a whole new road network. The contractors study the plans and work out how much to charge. Each contractor submits as low a tender as possible to try and win the contract. Sometimes a contractor draws up a different plan (called an alternative tender) to bring his price down further. Tenders for a motorway contract must be completed within twelve weeks.

Once a contract has been awarded, a DTp engineer (known as a Resident Engineer) is sent to the winning contractor to make sure all work is completed according to plan. In the picture below, the Resident Engineer for the Leatherhead/Wisley section of the M25 is seated at the end of the table. On either side are engineers from Fairclough Civil Engineering. They are all discussing a relief map of the route on the table. Behind them is a flat plan of the same section.

# Buying the land

Long before any work can begin, the DTp must buy all the land needed to build the different sections of the motorway. Much of it is private farmland, like that shown below. The DTp appoints an independent valuer to work out how much the land is worth. A price is fixed and the farmer is paid in full. This kind of purchase is called a compulsory purchase.

Later on, DTp surveyors arrive to check the ground level. If the land is too uneven, it will have to be smoothed out. This engineer is using a surveying instrument called a level. It consists of a small telescope attached to a three-legged stand called a tripod. While the surveyor looks through the telescope, his assistant stands a few metres away, holding up a kind of long ruler called a staff. The surveyor notes where the horizontal line of sight inside the telescope meets the metre scale on the staff. The point where they meet shows the height of the land on which the assistant is standing. Another reading taken a few metres further on will show whether the land is sloping up or down.

Once all the preparatory work has been completed, the land now belonging to the DTp is fenced off. This is done very accurately to avoid arguments with the owners of neighbouring pieces of land.

# Site offices

Work starts on the site offices. The offices for the Leatherhead/Wisley section were built on farmland bought specially for that purpose. They took only a few days to erect. Most of the sections were delivered to the site ready-made. The workmen simply fitted them together.

Inside the offices, there is room for two teams of engineers – one employed by Fairclough's, the other by the DTp. The two teams work side by side, the first supervising and carrying out the actual building of the motorway; the second checking that all work has been done correctly. The offices also house a laboratory where soil, concrete and other material samples can be tested, as well as a canteen, showers and lavatories for the staff.

Fairclough's engineers work closely with the company's Project Manager (also known as the Agent). It is the Agent's job to make sure that all workers and materials arrive on time, and that each stage of work is completed satisfactorily. He is also responsible for discussing progress with the Resident Engineer, and writing regular reports for his colleagues at head office.

# Land clearance

Before any building work can begin, the land has to be cleared of all obstacles, both natural and man-made. A large contractor, such as Fairclough's, usually does this itself. A smaller contractor will often employ a specialist firm to do it instead. This kind of agreement is called a subcontract.

However, if a large area of woodland is to be felled, even a major contractor may use professional tree-fellers to clear the land. The tree-fellers may take part of their fee as timber, and then sell it to customers of their own. Any wood that cannot be used is burned on site.

Unlike smaller roads, motorways are only linked to other roads at specially built junctions. This means that when a motorway is being built, the normal traffic flow is not interrupted. But when work starts on a junction or a bridge, the contractor must make sure that the roadworks cause as few hold-ups as possible. This may mean building entirely new stretches of road to divert the traffic from the work area. Special signs are put up to warn motorists of the diversion.

# Preparing the ground

Large earth-moving machines start removing the top layer of soil, known as topsoil. In open areas, twin-engined scraper tractors move more than 30 cubic metres of soil at a time. The topsoil is heaped up nearby. Later, it will be spread on the motorway embankments and planted with grass.

Scraper tractors are also used to level out the ground on which the motorway will be built. The tractors remove all earth above the planned route and transport it to lower 'fill' areas. Some earth is sold to local farmers. They spread it on low-lying fields to help prevent flooding.

Back-acting excavators are preferred where space is limited. A kind of large bucket, fixed to a long metal arm, scoops up the soil and tips it into a dump truck.

In a 'fill' area, the earth is deposited in layers, each approximately 30 centimetres thick. The earth is then rolled flat.

This is done with a bulldozer fitted with special compactor wheels. The compacted soil is built up to the height needed to allow road construction to begin. The ground on which the first layer of motorway is built is called the subgrade.

# Materials

A motorway must be very strong to carry the thousands of vehicles which travel on it each day. To give it strength, it is built in three main layers – the capping layer (at the bottom), the sub-base, and the surface layer, which may be formed from concrete or tarmacadam. The choice of surface depends partly on the building materials available nearby. Between Leatherhead and Wisley, the surface is concrete.

All concrete is made from a mixture of gravel (called aggregates), sand, cement and water. Aggregates often have to be transported to the site from a gravel pit some distance away. This is both costly and time-consuming. But if there is a local gravel pit, the contractor may be able to quarry its own aggregates. Huge cranes scoop out the material, still mixed with soil, and load it into trucks.

The trucks carry the aggregates to a washing and screening plant. Here the sand and gravel is cleaned and separated. The gravel stones are sorted according to size. Different sizes of stones are needed for making different types of concrete.

Concrete is produced at a batching plant. Different types of concrete are made by mixing varying amounts of each material. Each kind of concrete is made for a particular purpose. Low strength 'lean mix' concrete is used for the motorway sub-base; strong 'pavement quality' concrete is used for surfacing.

# The sub-base

A capping layer is placed on the subgrade to provide a strong base for the new road. It consists of gravel and sand, sometimes mixed with a small amount of cement for added strength. The dry cement is piped into a spreader from a cement tanker.

The mixture is rolled and left to harden. Rolling helps to remove air pockets, so making the material denser and stronger. Further layers are added until the capping reaches the correct thickness. The thickness depends on how strong the road needs to be to support the traffic which will use it.

The sub-base is made from lean mix concrete. The concrete is supplied semi-dried and laid with an automatic paver. On the Leatherhead/Wisley section, Fairclough's developed a new method of paving which enabled them to lay the sub-base much more quickly than is usual.

Once the lean mix concrete is rolled to the correct thickness, a special black liquid, called a sealant, is sprayed onto the concrete. This helps the concrete stay moist long enough to set without cracking. In the bottom right-hand corner of the picture, you can see how the sub-base has been built up.

# The paving train

The final top layer of concrete, called pavement quality concrete, is laid by a nine-piece 'paving train'. This enormous machine, over 50 metres long, moves along specially-built rails, spreading wet concrete evenly over the sub-base. It lays half a kilometre per day.

On the Leatherhead/Wisley section, the paving train was supplied with concrete from Fairclough's own batching plant. The concrete was delivered by relays of specially built side-tipping trucks. When required, a truck simply tipped its container sideways and poured the concrete into a spreader funnel on the front section of the train.

The concrete is laid in four strips, known as 'rips'. In this picture, the paving train is completing the final rip. The channel of earth beside it will become the central reservation, dividing the opposing streams of traffic. Every six metres, a 'crack inducer' is set into the concrete. Crack inducers ensure that the drying concrete cracks in a controlled pattern. Without them, the concrete might crack too irregularly to support the weight of traffic.

Once the concrete is laid, it is covered with tenting to protect it while it sets. On the left of this picture you can see two sections of tenting on a lorry.

# Bridge-building

When Fairclough's put in their tender for the Leatherhead/Wisley contract, they included separate estimates for thirteen bridges and viaducts. One was for a bridge to replace an old stone-built bridge over the River Mole.

Obviously, work on any bridge begins with its supports. The columns, or 'piers', must be strong enough both to carry the weight of the road, and the vehicles travelling along it. They are erected on deep foundations (called piles) to prevent them sinking into the ground. The piles for the bridge over the River Mole are made of reinforced concrete cased in steel.

Reinforced concrete is used when a structure needs to be particularly strong. It is made by pouring liquid concrete over a framework of steel rods, and then leaving the concrete to set. The design of the framework depends on how strong the reinforced concrete needs to be. The steel in this picture will be used as reinforcement for the underside of the bridge's carriageway (called the deck). It is being delivered by one of Fairclough's suppliers, who won the contract to provide all the steel needed for this section of the motorway.

The bridge's deck is built from extra-strong reinforced concrete to prevent it sagging between piers. Here you can see how closely the steel rods are meshed together.

# Surfacing

When all the steelwork is complete, liquid concrete is delivered to the bridge by concrete-mixer. For a large bridge like this, the concrete is pumped into a long flexible tube, by a machine called a concrete feed pump. It is spread directly onto the steel mesh. A workman guides the end of the delivery tube to make sure the concrete is spread evenly.

Meanwhile, another workman guides a smaller tube, called a poker vibrator, through the wet concrete. The vibrations force air bubbles in the concrete to rise to the surface, and help the concrete to settle or 'compact'. In this way, the concrete becomes thicker and stronger.

Once the concrete has compacted, a wooden board (called a screed) is pulled across the surface to give it a smooth finish. A perfect result is achieved with the help of a steel float, guided by hand.

# Old and new

When the concrete has set, the bridge is coated with special waterproofing material to protect it from damage. Without such protection, the bridge's steel and concrete framework would soon begin to rust and crumble.

Finally, the bridge's crash barriers are erected. These must not only suit the design of the bridge but, more importantly, be strong enough to prevent vehicles falling off it.

After several months' hard work, the bridge is finally complete. You can see a picture of it on the right. Below is a picture of the old bridge, taken from exactly the same position. Notice how heavy the old bridge's arches look, and how they block the river's flow. By comparison, the new bridge is light and graceful, offering uninterrupted views on all sides.

# Completion

Since the first motorway was built in the 1950s, people have become much more aware of the need to protect the countryside. As a result, new roads are being designed to cause as little damage to the environment as possible. In the case of the M25, this has even meant digging a tunnel to preserve a beautiful old cricket pitch in Epping Forest!

These embankments have been built up with topsoil kept for this purpose. The soil is being sprayed with a mixture of straw, grass seed and fertiliser. The white strands of fibreglass shown in the foreground will help to prevent the seed being washed away by the rain. In a few months' time, the embankments will be covered with grass and wild flowers.

Meanwhile, other workmen are erecting crash barriers down the central reservation, and painting lane division markings on the carriageway. For safety reasons it is important to make all signs as clear as possible. Vehicles travel at such high speeds on motorways that accidents are often serious.

Electricians are connecting up the emergency telephones on the hard shoulder (the outside edge of the carriageway). There is one telephone every kilometre. Motorists can use a telephone to call for help if their vehicle breaks down.

# Open to traffic

In November 1984, the Leatherhead/Wisley section of the motorway was opened to traffic. It had been completed in just under $2\frac{1}{2}$ years. There was no formal opening ceremony. The sign boards to the motorway were simply uncovered and the road blocks taken away.

Like every other section of the M25, the Leatherhead/Wisley section became immediately popular with commercial and private motorists alike. It is now used by lorry and truck drivers travelling west to join the M3 or M4, or east to Dover and the continent. Commuters use it to cut their travelling time to work, and families use it on their way to the countryside or the sea.

In fact the M25 has proved so popular that travellers on some sections are being delayed by traffic jams. It is already clear that much of the motorway will have to be widened before the end of the century – and some sections well before that.

Even so, the motorway has cut the amount of traffic travelling in and out of London; and it has linked areas which were once several hours' travelling apart. It has also given a boost to the construction industry, providing perhaps as many as 50,000 jobs over the last twenty years. Now the M25 is complete, the industry must greet the possibility of motorway widening contracts with some relief. It is unlikely that many other major motorway-building contracts will be open to bids in the near future.

# Index